Disclaimer

Let me start with the disclaimer- this book has been entirely made up as a practical joke to annoy my brothers and friends- do not attempt to extract anything useful from this book bar laughter at their expense. If there is useful information in here it was completely accidental. The book is grammatically poor and not well written (Dan helped me). Apologies to anyone whom this describes a little too accurately- it's coincidental... or is it?

Dedications/Thanks

It is a common known fact that anyone with a name like Carl, Dan, Mark, Rob, Sam or Tom have a smaller than average penis. I know a Carl, a Dan and a Tom who have struggled with this all their lives and I am tired of them feeling so ashamed of it. I have written a book full of advice and guidance on how to enjoy life regardless. I got most of this advice from the above named guys.

(it is definitely not from me, mine is massive).

Essentially- I have written this book for my 5 brothers and a couple of my smaller equipped best friends.

Thank you to my wife for putting up with me. She is a legend, has an even worse sense of humour and is currently working on our second kid!

Thank you to my daughter for putting up with me as a Dad and for never reading this heinous literature.

Sorry Mum, I know you won't find this funny- Dad, I know you will. I promise to publish a more serious book in the future.

Contents

Introduction: learning to live large… figuratively…

So, size is an issue.. or is it? The answer is yes, it is, for most things men do- for example you couldn't use your penis to strangle an attacking thief, itch your knees or choke a dog (Tom said he tried that once) but you most certainly can procreate- Carl, Dan and Tom have children. Since the penis was invented to make children and be played with, and since both of these can be done regardless of size, I would say you can still live it large.

What does this mean? well it means that first of all you are normal and able to do what we, as men, are born to do. Some people may have described the Dan I know as having "an innie for a penis" or him having a "mangina" but what those men didn't know is that Dan had already stuck his whole 2 inches into their mum.

The rest of this book is going to teach you how to be happy, and even proud, as you are- by utilising the many stories I have heard from Carl, Dan, Mark, Rob, Sam and Tom- and how they have learned to love little, and live large.

Chapter 1: "Fun size Adventures"

There are many situations where having a smaller than average sized penis comes in handy-
Carl, for example, likes to sneak into feminist events for all the great food they serve. At the door to many of these events, you have to pull down your trousers and prove you are a woman- for me, or the person who bought you this book- that would likely be impossible- but Carl can easily cover his package with a little vagazzle or a nice Brazilian hair trim. In he goes without a care in the world, and smile on his face, to the some of the world's cleanest events.

Some people- such as my brother Tom- have a strange habit of getting an erection whenever they feel nervous, scared or excited. Tom has confessed to me at getting erections at funerals, whilst on the bus, when angry in traffic and at family gatherings (though he said that was for other reasons).
Now if that was me, I would be knocking mourners over, tripping up travellers, blocking my windscreen or getting banned from family scrabble nights- but for you and him- it's just not a problem. Tom smiles away in the knowledge his 3 inches are solid, unseen, and but a few inches from Nan.

I put out a survey to the "big men, small problems" society for some feedback on their small problems. Many of them instead replied that they love being well below average and so here are some of the replies:

Mark's reply was that he loved that he had to be more inventive in the bedroom. He said as an engineer he would never think of the cup as more empty or full- but that the cup was the wrong size. With this in mind he found that most condoms fit a couple of his ogre sized fingers better anyway.

Dan replied to the survey with an email titled "get a better job". He wrote at length, utilising terrible spelling and grammar, about how I was only his friend. He went on to also explain that his wife was smarter than him and he hated that. Since Dan is mostly computer illiterate- I assume he accidentally lifted a page from his digital diary and emailed me that instead of a reply.
(Dan regularly boasts of having an iQ of 75).. questionable.

Rob and Sam wrote back that their favourite thing about having a smaller penis is that they fit comfortably into their partners sleek and silky underwear. When welding or working the farm they don't worry about chaffing or sweating- their only concern is that they may have slightly stretched their wives lingerie.

OFFICIAL THUMB'S UP FROM ALL ROB'S AND SAM'S 
* ALSO ELECTRICIAN'S, DESIGNER'S, PLUMBER'S, ARCHITECT'S AND VEGAN'S *

The main point to this being that none of these weirdos have let their tiny wieners change them as people or influence them for the worse. They were already terrible people. They have however learned to utilise their uniqueness to their benefit. There are hundreds of benefits or examples of things you can do that your well-endowed counterparts cannot. I will list a few now:

- ☐ You won't accidentally scare anyone on nudist beaches.

- ☐ You are unlikely to block the airway of your significant other.

- ☐ You can fly, run and ski better due to a more streamlined structure.

- ☐ You can measure the snow depth in places like Spain.

- ☐ Less surface area for your herpes and friction burns to affect you.

☐ You spend much less on willy warmers.

- ☐ Your arms get less tired when wanking.

- ☐ Your balls are easier to shave around.
  Please be even more careful with the shaver

- ☐ Your testicles will always look massive.

- ☐ There is less chance of your cat mistaking your weenus for a cat toy… Though you do need to fear birds. More reasons to get a cat.

- ☐ More sex position possibilities- the "reverse cold", "belly button bang" and the "violent earbud" to name a few.

- ☐ Always accessible and free fishing bait. (Small fish)

- ☐ Your penis won't touch the church pew when attending a wedding in a kilt. That's not fun.

- ☐ An erection whilst rock climbing won't push you off the wall/rocks.

- ☐ That weird fish in the amazon rainforests that can swim up your urethra when you pee in the rivers should have a harder time attacking you. Those fish are real- look it up.

CAN YOU FIT IN?
NOPE!?
HAVE YOU SEEN MY WIFE?

- ☐ Incredible accuracy is required to dick shot you whilst playing cricket or football.

- ☐ You are unlikely to disappoint your family by entering the porn industry.

- ☐ You don't have to worry about the famed "steroid shrinkage" conundrum

- ☐ You will never accidentally touch toilet water with your penis when say having a poo.

- ☐ You use less body wash in the shower.

Maybe take this opportunity to think about the good that has come from having your penis just the way it is- or being you knowing you have your penis. You never need to worry that your partner is with you just for your dick. It's just the normal things people worry about like your money. There is good- so before starting the next chapter- think about that good. Think small and hard.

Chapter 2: "In the Defence of dicks"

So here's the thing- size is subjective. Compared to me- Carl, Dan and Tom may look like they brought a maggot to a snake fight but compared to a 5 year old- they have a Moby dick (the whale not the singer).

If you are 3 to 4 feet tall, a 3 to 4 inch penis is an ok ratio to look normal. I would say a foot of height per inch of penis is probably a good guess of what an adequate body to penis ratio looks like

Size averages also change according to country. If size bothers you- move to where you are above average.
Here is a list of a few countries where you could pull out your wang as a party trick and impress people:

Thai, Cambodian and North Korean penis' are, on average, below 4inch/10cm. This is actually true.
So book yourself a relatively cheap flight and go and entice some locals.

Sam- from the "big men, small problems" society- has said that moving to Cambodia wouldn't help him as when erect he maxes out at 1.5inches. What he also said was that he has found a niche fetish group called "Tight Arses". Tight Arses is a collective of men and women who are rich and have small arseholes- plus they love anal- That is a hole Sam knew he could fill.

Sam at a recent Tight Arses meet up

Dan's penis used to be above average.
Fortunately a freak accident involving a bet and a horse cut his penis down to 2 inches. I say fortunately as his favourite past time pre accident was autofellatio. Due to losing the ability autofellatio Dan dedicated his time to developing his tongue skills in and out of the bedroom and he is now a pro whistler. It doesn't pay much- but his version of "spice up your life" by the spice girls is fantastic. Whilst most people would assume that Dans confidence would have taken a hit after the accident- it didn't. The horse he assaulted before the accident was owned by a lovely woman whom he found very attractive. Post-accident and on his first whistle tour- Dan returned to the farm to apologise to the horse and decided to pluck up the courage to ask the woman out- they have been together ever since.

When I quizzed Dan about plucking up the courage to ask his now wife out- he said before his accident he was so obsessed with sucking his own penis he barely had time to think about anything else. After injury Dan had to develop other hobbies and look for new meaning. He has become a better man due to having his manhood savagely cut short. He realised boasting about his penis previously was more a sign of deep rooted insecurity- like driving a car with a loud exhaust- and that once the ability to boast had gone he addressed the root of those insecurities and became more confident in himself.

MOMENTS BEFORE AN
INNOCENT HORSE WAS ASSAULTED
DAN, WOULD YOU RATHER SUCK OFF A HORSE, OR GET SUCKED OFF BY ONE?
GET SUCKED OFF, HAVE YOU SEEN A HORSES DICK?!
YEAH, BUT HAVE YOU SEEN A HORSES MOUTH?

This horrific and completely factual story about Dan may be hard to read- but the confidence element is a game changer. Being able to be confident, regardless of size, will help you into the bed of the girlfriends, wives, sisters, mothers or fathers of those that would laugh at your penis.

When you think about it, really, having a massive penis isn't actually great for too many things. The fact I have a full body workout trying to wrestle mine into the toilet when I need a piss isn't always the best way to start the day. I spend twice as much on body wash and I always knock my bell end on coffee tables and short chairs.

"Tiny houses" was 2018's biggest social media trend! I think most people love the idea of modular living and a house made of shipping containers in the woods. Why not make "tiny penises" the biggest trend of 2024? "All homes must have a little one", "go small or go home" or "travel size for convenience" are some examples of lines you could use to start the trend.

Show yourself off- stop being shy about it. Get on onlymans, get yourself a camera with adequate zoom and get some extra cash in- you may want some for our next chapter?

Chapter 3: "Tiny Tools, Big Tricks"

By now you are starting to realise It's not all doom and gloom for you and your tiny penis. Sometimes it really is though (I imagine). So let's look at what some guy do to get the max out of their mini.

I am sure most of you are like Tom. Tom struggles to satisfy his partner sexually due to his size.
(penis and chest muscles).
Luckily for you and him, there are options.

Padded penis, from padded penis limited, is a company that Tom started on the side to get the most out of his manhood. He has invented a condom that is padded to add to your size and impact- a bit like chicken fillets for women. Since there isn't much for it to fit to- it doubles as an incontinence pad that you squeeze between your arse cheeks. Tom says it helps with the fact that he often shits himself when cries- and he always cries when he orgasms. It is a viscous cycle.

If padded penis isn't for you (not sponsored content) then there are various other options available- there is a complete lack of science behind most of the following suggestions- but Carl, Dan, Mark, Rob, Sam and Tom have tried them anyway.

Over the next few pages I will give you an overview of a few of them.

Rob personally told me that he is part of a religion that believes that there is a big penis inside of everyone. This religion, aptly named Willigion, pray to their lord Meatus by pulling hard on each other's pieces each Sunday at their weekly meetings. Some Willigioner's claim to see growth of up to 10% a year- though there have been injuries to some of the more extreme of the religion who call themselves "the members".

Carl, famed adrenaline junkie and lover of heights, has found a different way to try and increase his length. Have you heard of the "slamming the door method" for removing wobbly teeth? well Carl has adapted that to try to extract more of his hidden inner penis- it hasn't worked much yet- but most of us who know him just believe he has become a bit of a masochist.

Sam the designer has told us his fun inflatable factory is where the real magic happens. Alongside all manner of inflatable sex toys he personally tests before sale- purely for quality assurance purposes- he has helped develop their famous and patented inflatable phallic. A short operation is required to install it, during which a potentially medically trained Dr inserts a small inflatable balloon into your penis. A valve is also hidden behind your nut sack. Your partner can then inflate at will, or if you are single- you can buy a pump adapter and peacefully play alone.

Dan said, alongside his whistling career, he also got into shadow puppetry post horse accident. A well placed torch balanced on his stomach can give Dan a pretty large shadow. He then takes pictures of these inflated silhouettes and sells them on only fans to magicians. He has lots of tiny penis costumes for his shadow puppetry including: a crocodile outfit, 007 and his favourite- a foot outfit. Dan famously LOVES feet almost as much as he loves magic.

Though many of these options only apply to you if you aren't happy with how you are- even though you should be. Whether you are or aren't- help picking up a partner wouldn't go amiss (if that's what you are looking for)- so since the subjects of this book are all married- I figured they must know some great pickup lines. Here are some of the examples of lines that worked for them:

- ☐ "Ever had a wet willy.. with an actual willy?"
  ~Rob

- ☐ "Fancy seeing who can drink the most tonight?"
  ~Carl

- ☐ "Hi, I'm Dan, I am a millionaire" (he isn't)
  ~Dan

- ☐ "30 ton polar bear, it breaks the ice"
  ~Sam

- ☐ "Roses are red, my penis is tiny, but that will be ok, in your tight behindy"
~Tom

- ☐ "Hi, I'm Sam, my friends a millionaire" (he isn't)
~Sam

- ☐ "I'm a welder" (always works)
~Mark

- ☐ "If I was to ask you out- would the answer to that question be the same as the answer to this question?" (Also always works)
~ Me

- ☐ "Are you my little toe? As I want to bang you on my coffee table this evening"
~Carl

- ☐ "I wanna tell your urethra it's nice to meet ya"
~Dan
(original lyrics from his upcoming rap and whistle album)

- ☐ "I would love a tickle of your little nipple"
~Rob

- ☐ "I drive a range rover sport"
~Sam

- ☐ "Look how long my tongue is!"
  ~Mark

- ☐ "How does a farmer get a girlfriend? A tractor"
  ~Sam

- ☐ "Have you ever been a car crash? Because I would love to rear end you!"
  ~Dan

- ☐ "Oh my god, your eyes are beautiful- oh wait- it's my reflection in them!"
  ~Tom

- ☐ "Let me just smell your hair"
  ~Carl

- ☐ "I'm a designer" (Works on furries)
  ~Sam

- ☐ "Fancy a finger?"
  ~Carl

- ☐ "Wanna shag?"
  ~Rob

☐   "Are you a mirror? Because I see myself in you" ~Sam

☐   "You look like my mum, and I would like to come out of you like I came out of her" ~Dan

If these don't work for you then your problem isn't your penis or the quality of the chat up lines, it is your delivery- but that is a different books problem.

Who am I kidding, most of these are scarily bad but worked anyway. If that doesn't boost your confidence I don't know what will. This group of small dicked dicks managed to meet and marry a women with terrible pick-up lines and tiny Tim's- so you definitely can.

....

On the following page there is a comparison chart of all penis' featured in this book. If the previous pages didn't make you feel better about your virtually non-existent sex tool- then this next one will.

SAM 1
CARL
SAM 2
TOM
ME (SOFT)
MARK
DAN
ROB
TRACINGS OF THE OUTLINES OF EACH PENIS FEATURED IN THIS BOOK (WHILE HARD)
THESE HAVE BEEN PRINTED IN ACTUAL SIZE SO YOU CAN COMPARE YOUR LITTLE LOVE TOOL.

Chapter 4: "The Art of Self"

"The art of self-love" was the title of Dan's autobiography (sorry for borrowing Dan). Whilst self-love is important, granted- not in the way Dan performed it, the art of self is more: Acceptance. Understanding. Progression.

As strange as it may be, self-love and self-acceptance are very important. By self-love, I am not referring to wanking, I couldn't possibly suggest that when Mark is 3 months sober of wanking to power rangers porn. What I am referring to is self-acceptance. Acceptance that YOUR penis is small and that is ok. Good.. almost. Carl. Dan. Mark. Rob. Sam. Tom. You have SMALL penis'.
Small for a prepubescent chimpanzee, never mind a full grown man. But that is ok. We all know it, so there is no need to be ashamed, embarrassed or scared.
Once you have accepted it- you can start to develop true happiness rather than "HA ... Penis"- which you are used to hearing.

When I explained the concept of happiness coming from within to Sam- he immediately agreed. He explained how he found his g-spot at a particularly devout Willigion meeting that Rob took him to. He then went on in detail at length how he struggled to derive pleasure from his 7cm penis, but has found a fortune of it 12cm up his brown tunnel. After his explanations and demonstrations, that I tried to avoid, I told him I was referring to more a sense of satisfaction, self-actualisation and clarity, not a physical pleasure or getting cum.. within. I still do not think he understood me- but that's ok- you do you Sam. If it makes you happy, it makes me happy.

Mark, Rob and Sam are the focus of Anita Camdoons book all about anger, so me telling them to be happier didn't really work. Mark tried to strangle me, Rob smashed a plate on my head then ran away shouting "dickhead" and Sam just started crying. He does that a lot- now there is a man in touch with his emotions. All the wrong ones- but he is in touch with them.

Tom was easy to approach about self-improvement, acknowledgement and understanding- as he runs his own gym. Unfortunately like most gym lovers- he is isn't very clever- but he can lift heavy stuff.
I used this simple metaphor to try to get Tom to love his undersized penis more-
Will lifting little weights lots make you as strong who lifts big weight less? He said that it would. It would just take longer.

This relates to how to please your partner sexually. A big dick may please your significant other easier and quicker- but if you take your time, a tiny penis can do the same thing.

Unfortunately for Tom, he has a disease called "instafinishosis". As soon as he touches his wife's genitalia- he finishes instantly. He is the only known person to have this frightful disease. It should give most other people a reason to smile though- your penis can still do its job- even if its "Tom long"- a famous term often used to describe tiny penis'.

I did recommend various methods to help combat his condition- ways to help him, and you, last longer and so give you the time to please your partner. Unfortunately- the "think of a relative" option only turned Tom on more- so I gave him some other ideas.

Sam has tried desensitising himself to sex by watching copious amounts of porn- however this just spurned an addiction that would spur a rather unappealing reputation. I wouldn't recommend this route as it sometimes makes you look for an unrealistic version of sex. Especially the stuff Sam was into.

I mentioned above about thinking about something or someone else- this can be a good option- but don't do a Carl and shout out the wrong name when finishing- especially not the family priest as Carl did- this may give your partner the wrong idea.

Removing your foreskin may have a few benefits- alongside a generally cleaner penis- your bell end can end up slightly desensitised to touch compared to its covered counterparts- this allowing for a longer last. Dan said this may be one of the few sexual benefits to having most of his dick bit off by a horse. He now lasts much longer.

Chapter 5: "Laughing Off The Banter"

"Regardless of whether you are hetro or LGBTQ+ there comes a time when you are surrounded by big dicks... that's when it's hardest" -Carl referencing how he has been mocked before in locker rooms.
Sometimes a good ribbing is hard to take- and as I have never been mocked I feel ill equipped to advise in this area- so I asked the usual suspects what they knew on how to laugh it off or get past when the vultures come at your slim pickings.

So moving forward we will have a look at a few ways to get through the phasing, bullying or mocking of your peers. Sometimes with humour, sometimes with sense. Sometimes pure rage.

I have referenced how Dan has slept with close relatives of bullies. That way, when they mocked him... he knew, deep down inside- that the family member that kisses them on the forehead at night... had kissed Dan in places I dare not write about. So who wins in the end?
No-one to be honest. But Dan doesn't lose- and that is a Dan motto. 10 points to Dan.

Sometimes you may prefer to draw attention to something else- this is a trick that Mark and Rob use. They just tell the would be verbal assaulters that they are vegan (which they are) and quite often the bullies are either too disgusted to mock them- or forget all about the fact that they were bullying them for having tiny dicks. It is all about misdirection. "Missed erection" Mark and Rob said- it's their term for misdirecting people from their penises'.

Sometimes security is better found in groups. It often is not hard to find out which of your foes is secretly hiding their own size related woes. Or just identifying others in the area who understand your pain or will support you. If you look up and down yourself you may recognise a few of these clear indicators that you have a tiny penis (apart from the tiny penis) these also help you identify others- let's look at a few now:

- ☐ You drive a car with a loud exhaust, and tiny engine. This is a direct metaphor for your loud mouth.. and tiny dick.

- ☐ You have tribal tattoos. Tattoos are art.. art is subjective. But everyone agrees- unless you are in a tribe- tribal tattoos indicate a lack of blood to your penis.

- ☐ Claiming to be "bald by choice" when… you aren't. Being bald is not a sign- claiming to not be bald is. Tiny dick. 100%.

- ☐ Wearing wax jackets or a chequered shirts/jeans combo are all definite signs of a smaller than average penis.

- ☐ A sign of a micro penis (1 inch or shorter) is that new type of man bag wannabe "gangstas" and actual teenagers wear across their chest.. needs no further explanation. Get your bum bags back out dads from the 80s, they are back in "style".

- ☐ Anybody who says or wears anything that says "gang" or "hood" on it... or wears their trousers lower than their arse. Without being in a gang, from a hood and showing off their arse because it is really good. You have clearly got a tiny penis. Trying to disguise it- we know.

- ☐ Anybody who constantly has their hands in their underwear... we know why- you are trying to check your dick is still there. It is, it's just really really really really small. Likely confused with a stiff pube.

- ☐ Puffer jackets. Not only weird looking. Sweaty looking. But also shows clear signs of weak/wasted away muscles and a completely unused tiny penis.

- ☐ T-shirts with pictures of half-naked men/women on them... nice misdirection- but we know what it means...

- ☐ Stealing a friend's baby name idea.. just... yeah. Everyone knows who you are. Name thief. Tiny penis.

- ☐ You drive well below the speed limit, brake excessively around corners or when there are oncoming vehicles or tailgate people. You clearly just want to either delay arriving at your destination or want to crash- in both cases it is because you think there is less chance people will see your little dick. We can see it anyway. It's on your forehead for all to see.

☐ You ride a pushbike to the front of a traffic queue at traffic lights. Then set off painfully slowly. Or just ride a pushbike for pleasure. Commuting is fine- save the planet- but get off the road at weekends. Those seats rub your penis away slowly- so we know yours is small.

☐ You "enjoy" running. Running as a mode of transportation is fine- but if you enjoy it- you are trying to run from the fact you have a tiny penis.

☐ You ride a motorbike. You may have absolutely massive balls, a lack of self-concern and general badass outward persona. But we see your inner insecurities and we see your little willy.

☐ You are the youngest, or second from youngest sibling- or an only child. All the good penis' are given to the older brothers- by the time the younger siblings are born, they get the little bits left over. If you have no siblings or an older sister- then unfortunately... you just have a tiny penis. Its science.

☐ You own a big dog, or more dogs than cats. Cats have big balls, dogs have big dicks. Your animal completes you. I have multiple cats and no dogs- so clearly I bring all the dick to the household. Count up your cat to dog ratio... yeah.... I told you. You have a small penis.

☐ You think anime is for kids. This not only shows a lack of understanding of an incredible artistic form of media- but also that you have a really small dick.

☐ Keyboard warriors. Needs no further information. Grow a dick.

☐ You have more male children than female children. This is a clear sign that nature feels the man of the household isn't man enough and so has taken steps to replace you and your tiny penis.

☐ You play games on an X not a PS or PC (legally cannot mention any brands- these are made up references to potential consoles that definitely do not exist). Regardless- Get a real console or real computer, not a shit version of both. Also, get a bigger dick, because yours is clearly minuscule.

☐ You wear tracksuits and gym wear at all times... and clearly do not exercise. You are pretending you are fit, and also pretending your penis is not tiny. It is. You have a tiny penis. We all know.

☐ You wear "sliders" or essentially "fashionable flip flops" with brand logos on- and you are not on a beach. Get a grip on your life mate- we know you can't get a grip on your penis. Its small.

- ☐ You are vegan or vegetarian- unless prompted by an allergy. There's a whole extra books worth of things this is a sign of- none of them are for saving the planet or animals. It's all about your penis. (Apologies to the tiny percentage of you who are trying to save animals or the planet).

- ☐ You don't know how to measure things properly. Clear sign of a tiny dick. For those of you whom this applies- measure your dick against this book- if it's as wide or shorter than this physical book when closed (5inches)- you have an average to small dick (that's ok). If your dick is as long as this book is tall (8inches)- then your dick is massive but still only half the size of mine. I know- it is a curse really.

- ☐ With the above in mind- if you are a lesser trade (plumber, electrician, carpenter, fitter, machinist, designer, painter or builder) and cannot at least vertical MMA weld... then you also cannot find your tiny penis.

- ☐ You have unwarranted bouts of incensed rage for no real reason. The real reason is your tiny penis, we know.

- ☐ You drop things like 'yeah man ya get me', 'bruv', 'tch' or 'Yeah im sorry for that but' the but being the complete erasure of anything pre-but. Also the erasure of any confusion about the fact your dick.. your dick be tiny.

- ☐ You drink alcohol and or smoke/vape on the regular, especially weed. My friend who is a Dr of engineering says this is how the following facts relate. The alcohol thins your blood, your penis inflates with blood, your penis gets thinner. Smoking shortens your lifespan, your penis makes life, your penis gets shorter when you smoke. Weed kills brain cells and makes your brain smaller, men think with their penis, ergo, your penis gets smaller alongside your brain. These are simple logical facts. A spliff or pint a day makes your penis go away- so the Dr's say.

- ☐ You drive slowly in the fast lane on the motorway. A sign of a stupidly small brain and immense arrogance... Oh, and a teeny tiny little dick.

Before we move on, it is likely that if you are a combination of points from above then you not only have the most nano dick of all- but you are also likely universally disliked.

If the following picture relates to you. I mean you too

So there you have it. Identify those others like yourself-group together- and never let a bully take you alone. Of course, you could always just dedicate multiple hours a week, or a day, to the gym to become massively hench. Or dedicate time to a martial art. That way no one will mock you anyway for fear of having their eyes popped out between your massive arms. I am talking to you Wayne- we know why you have all those muscles! You didn't think you would escape this did you?! Mwahaha.

Your final defences are either the self-confidence to not care for others opinions (as they don't actually matter anyway) or to develop enough humour to spin it round. A well timed joke can save you, and how you feel, whilst gently encouraging people to leave you alone as you are clearly much more intelligent than them.

A contradictory point is that when a smart person is arguing with a dumb person, from the outside, all it looks like is two dumb people arguing. So if you find yourself in a locker room or changing room getting mocked- just run in the other direction. No-one knows what to do when someone just... runs away. They aren't likely to chase you to hit you with their latest joke. Just don't forget your towel when you do.

The final note is that everyone feels like their dick is small sometimes (apart from me) so just talk about it with people. Keeping quiet won't do anything, so how you feel about it won't get any better. Shout from the rooftops if you need to- or confide in family:

'My name is .... And I HAVE A TINY PENIS!'

Draw a picture of yourself above to further embody truth.

Conclusion: "Living Large in a Small World"

What have we learned?

We have learned that your penis size should not impact your confidence, sexual ability or life in any negative way.

We have learned to identify others like Carl, Dan, Mark, Rob, Sam and Tom.

We have learned that I will write an entire book as a practical joke vs my brothers and friends. This is the first of a series of increasingly terrible idea's. All money made from this will be invested into more elaborate pranks.

And...

Well, it would be lovely if this book has either helped you feel better about your tiny penis, or made you laugh. Hopefully it hasn't made you feel worse- and it can at least help you identify your brothers in arms. But no matter what- I know that it has royally annoyed all my brothers and my friends- so I win regardless. Also I get paid if someone bought you this- so even if it was useless to you I made money. Let's get real though- this won't sell any copies- even though I put loads of effort into the drawings and everything. They took me ages! I am not as artistic as I was when I was a kid- plus I'm great with pencils or ball points- but I needed to do this on a tablet so it was digital to upload into the book. I was also in a rush to get it done by Christmas...

It's not like I'm not busy with other things- I have a busy
job, I'm a dad, a husband, I have another baby on the way,
I have decided to build my kitchen myself from scratch, I
need to sort the baby room and the bathroom, I'm starting
a gym equipment business, On that note I need to also
stay fit no one will buy gym equipment from me if I am fat,
I'm reliable so people always ask me for favours, I'm trying
to up my financial intelligence so in reading books ALL day
EVERY DAY, I'm insecure so I always answer the phone to
people and talk probably too long with them
unnecessarily, it's not like evenings or weekends are any
more free- if anything they are worse- top it all off with
the fact that post 30 my body is essentially held together
with stitches, medication and most likely lumps of weld
and silicone... it's just a lot... you know? Also, I'm
predominantly a lazy person that never has the time to be
lazy- but also I love gaming and anime so they need to
factor into my time and I need to have more holidays- my
wife has requested it multiple times and we do need one
to be honest it's been a long time and we deserve a break,
everyone deserves breaks or chances to do new stuff or
what's the point in being here you know what I'm saying?
Ugh, I don't know why I'm explaining this- no-one will read
this far, I could probably put my bank details right here in
this published book and no one would steal a penny. Then
again, there's no money left to steal now- this was an
expensive practical joke. I have to pay for a tablet and a
computer to get it all uploaded. I spent the family savings.
My wife is going to kill me... ugh... what have I done?!?!
Was it worth it? Well, was it?!!

... yeah... it was.

PushA BaLlin.

Disclaimer, again: Remember this book is intended purely for entertainment purposes, and its light-hearted tone is meant to bring a smile to readers' faces and a perk to your little penis. Similarities between you and this book are coincidental. If you don't like it, don't read it.

A final game:
        See if you can find some differences between the
                        following 2 images

DICK'S DO
LOVE A
BIT OF
FOOTY

DICK'S DO
LOVE A
BIT OF
TENNIS

Well done. Here is what your results mean:

If you found 1 difference:

You have a tiny penis.

If you found 3 differences or more:

You have a tiny penis,

You have no friends,

You smell like regurgitated poo juice.

If you couldn't find any differences:

You have a massive dick,

You have lots of friends,

You smell lovely,

You are intelligent, attractive and funny.

The end.

Other books coming soon:

'Why am I always angry'

By Anita Camdoon

A look into chronic fury and unwarranted rage.

'The Way of the Welder'

By Balian O'Fearth

An actual educational masterpiece about the various incredible knowledge bases and skill sets required to become a professional Welder.

More planned, but not named.. let's see how much trouble this book gets me in first.

Take some notes for yourself on the following blank pages:

www.ingramcontent.com/pod-product-compliance
Lightning Source LLC
Chambersburg PA
CBHW060846260726
48661CB00002B/641